Poison Apple

Megan Dhakshini

Published by Unsolicited Press
www.unsolicitedpress.com

Artwork provided by: Kitty Ritig, Sachin Raveena, Sindu Sivayogam (murukku), Sesha Nithyananthan, Minal Naomi, and Dillai Joseph.

Cover Art by: Mister Guns

For information, contact publisher at info@unsolicitedpress.com

Unsolicited Press Books are distributed by Ingram.
Printed in the United States of America.

ISBN: 978-1-947021-29-7

Contents

Some places, you can never leave.

Some places never leave you.

Poison Apple

You are the thing that I most desire

The thing that I just shouldn't want.

I'll need to want you as long as I mustn't,

As long as I know that I can't.

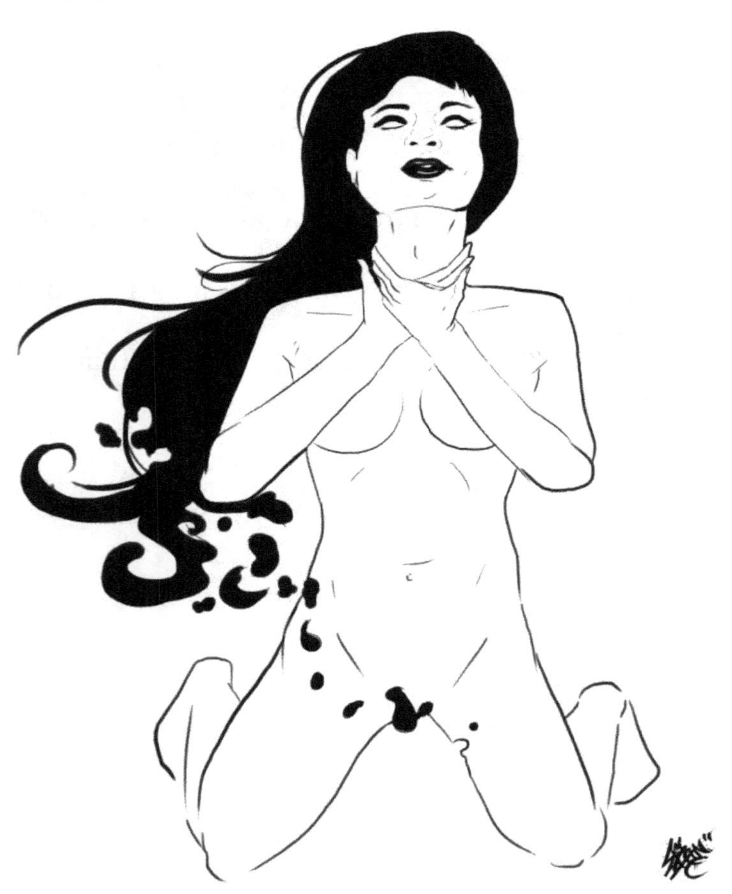

Her.

The temptress. The luscious apple.

Sometimes, I'd imagine brokenness

fluttering aimlessly inside her;

Shreds of colour & chaos;

Fragments of everything & nothing.

Destruction I could pick up, shake and peer at

through mirrored eyes.

She was my kaleidoscope girl; and I found peace

in her despair.

Raw. Glowing. Untamed.

Infinitely ethereal.

A goddess to those who could see her.

None could bear to reflect her true spirit;

Except he, who could lap up her flames-

feed her fire.

Raw. Wild. Fire.

She owned spaces;

Halls, lanes, stares on faces.

hissing tongues

and poisoned whispers.

Heartbreaker.

Breath-taker.

Stunner.

CRASH

Poetic Creature;

She wore star-lined eyes.

Her pockets,

Filled with raindrops,

crescent moons and whispers.

Goddamn Goddess;

She'd tether you to her hips,

curve her lips,

sing of sins, whims,

what-ifs and why-nots.

If you wanted to, you could

crash into love with her.

Every jagged shard and

molten dust of you

would wear star-lines too.

Poetic Creature;

Goddamn Goddess;

Woman.

Wild.

> Like the afterglow of a storm-kissed grassland.

> Like plunging avalanches of violence.

> Like savage tangles of charcoal black verse.

> Fierce, boisterous, beautifully wild hair.

And she was December mist;

And thunderstorms and rain.

And sometimes

she was, sunrises.

Him

The alpha. The poison.

Alpha

Eyes. That command open

minds, hearts, legs,

lips. That dictate whims,

wants, needs, no's,

strings. That pull back

from curves, thrusts, tears,

sins. That weigh down on his

stride, heart, mind

Eyes. That will make you sigh.

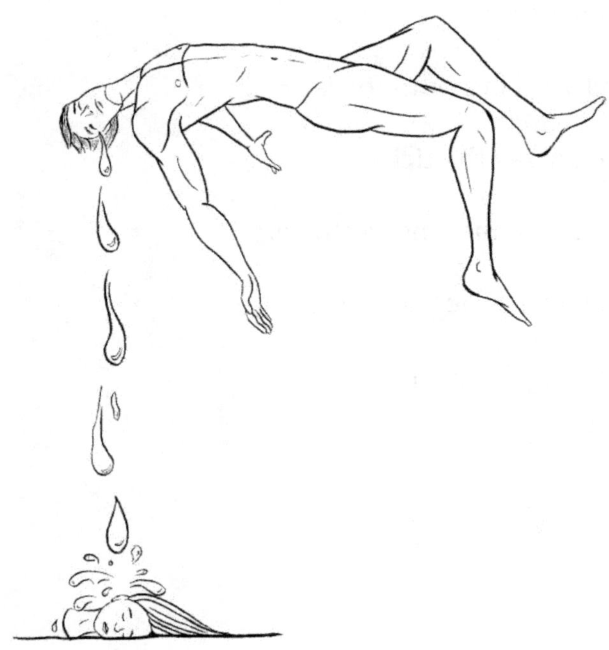

Prisoner of Time.

He hoarded timepieces,

  Like he hoarded regret.

Cold metal kisses

  Clasped with lassos of forget

He blinked away the ticks

  And glanced sometimes at tocks

"I'll watch over time" he thought

  "Till someday it's mine."

Soul

You see,

You are much too old.

Your river seeks canyons to carve.

Your melodies are not music. Not yet.

Your language is yet to be born.

You are of the Sea, the Earth, the Breeze.

You are Freedom. You are Free.

You see,

you are love, old soul.

But you are much too old, to see.

He could indulge in her all day.

Watch her.

Wear her.

Blink. Then come back to new discoveries.

Not because she was anything extraordinary.

But because He was.

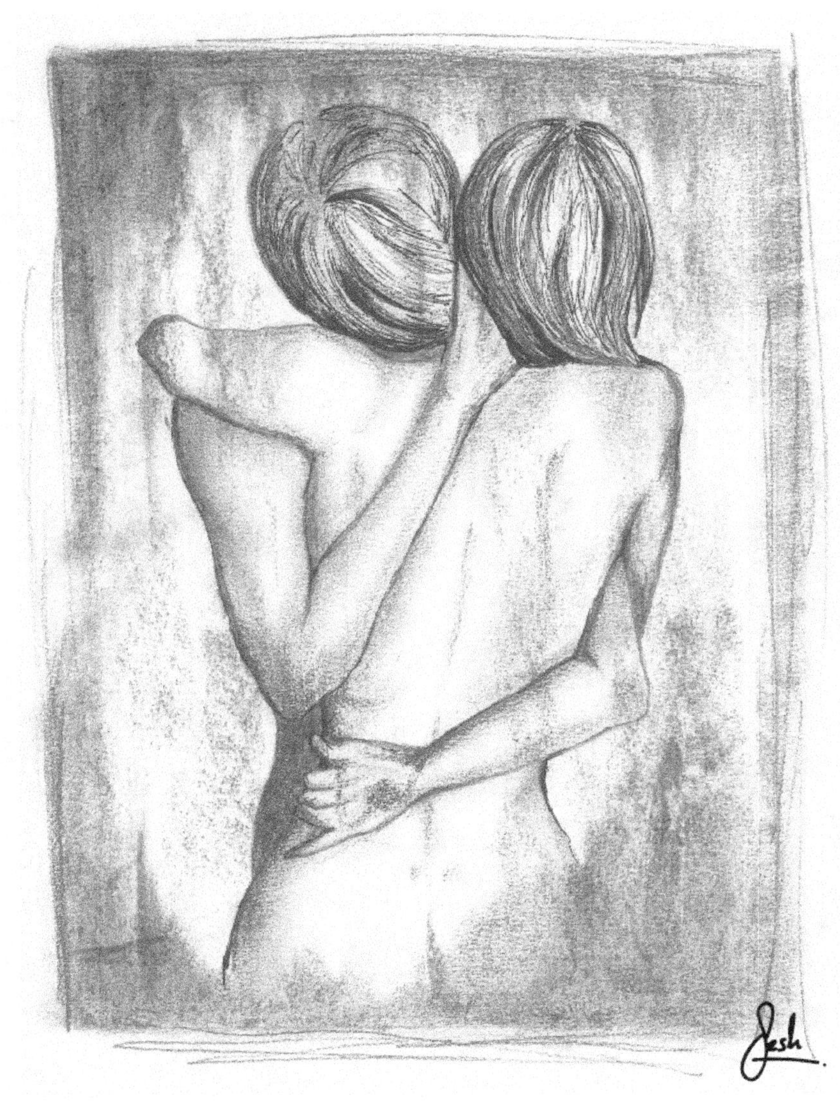

He blew out the candles

and watched the wax weep.

Another year of darkness,

another dream asleep.

He was left there, to wither,

The Unbreakable Man.

A pile of old nightmares,

Till love found him there

FULFILLED

The gaps in his existence;

Screaming slits on barbed wire fences.

But there she was, that chilling breeze;

She'd fill those gaps,

He'd let her bleed.

She was envious

of his

Once-upon-a-times,

And him,

Of her

Happily-ever-afters.

Hard to love

Harder to hate

Lips of gold

Heart of slate

Sometimes

being black

means you can

be written on,

be a starscape haven

give birth to moons.

Black like

your skin

your voice

and sometimes

your heart.

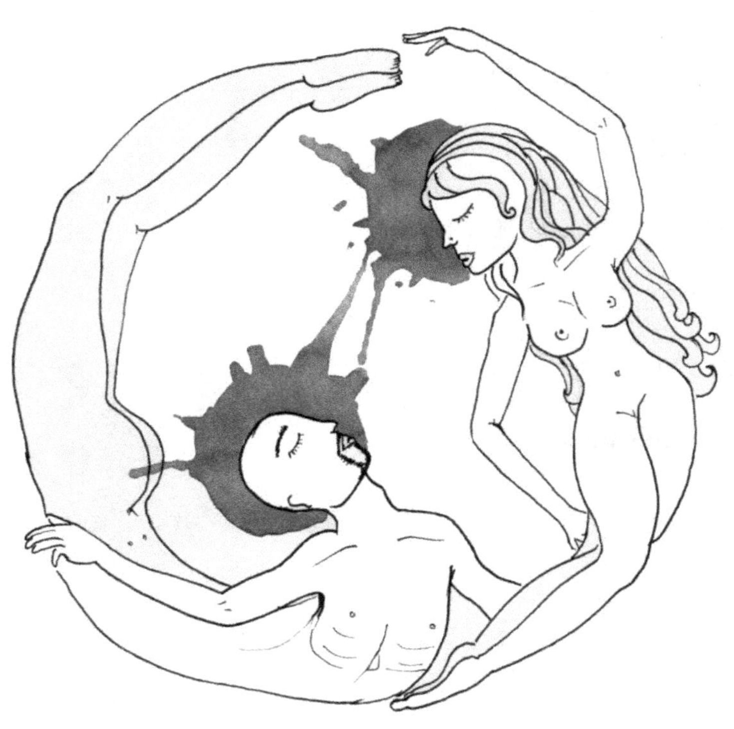

Them

The lust. The love. The bite.

OurPlay

Sinners:

Entangled,

in sweat, fingers, heaves,

in mirrors;

echoing rivers

of lamplight fighting through

fierce cracks in flesh;

Faces, watching faces,

watching mirrors,

bodies playing out parades,

commands, pauses, ;

watching mirrors,

watching back.

Temple of Sin

Sacred vice;

Sacrificial flesh.

Serpent, servant, sin;

The devil's own son with his offerings,

At her feet an alter builds.

Your words,

They do to me what

Fingers do to zips,

Clasps, buttons, lips;

Write to me.

Luna's love

Darkness,

My dear prince.

It pains me so

How the world forgets to know

How I glow

How I glow

How I glow.

Rain Soaked toes:

Denim scented Thighs;

Coffee stained lips.

Still,

I couldn't help but start with those eyes.

When we're finished,

I hope you're famished.

"Your soul is a song" He said.

"Only because you know exactly how to string the notes

together" She smiled.

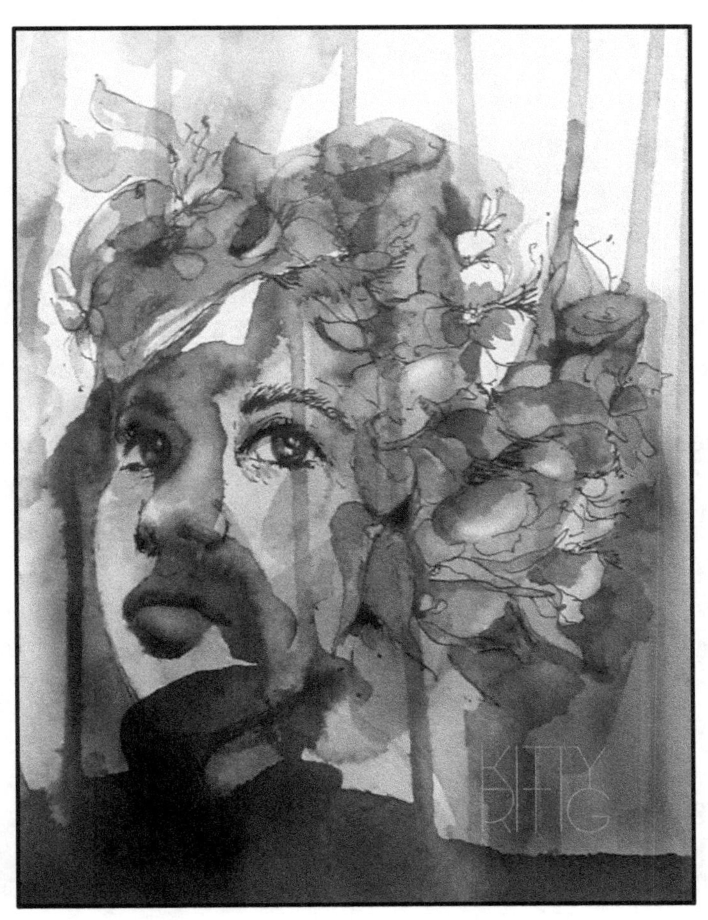

Black magic blushed her cheeks and filth lines her eyes a

murky charcoal. There were dimples in the folds of her skin,

left behind by drunken smiles he traced on her with ravenous

fingers.

He was meat. gluttony. dirt.

Afterglows were beautiful, she thought,

only because they were not.

Come closer

Collide with me

Undo my night.

Come closer

Melt into me

Turn the darkness hot white

Come closer

Hell's missing me-

The goddess must sin to survive.

Where does your smile linger, when it fails to find my eyes?

I tried never to love her ordinarily.

I needed to savour her-like that last shred of crackling on a

winter dinner plate. I wanted the distant lure of that fantasy

walk in a Sicilian spring. The adventure of tasting the

luscious morsel of a poison apple. The lusty longing for dark

places.

I tried never to love her ordinarily.

That would mean accepting that she was real.

Home,

Is every secret story

My skin remembers.

Take me home.

Let me undress you.

You.

Pre-loved possession;

Hand-me-down hornets nest;

Second-hand celebration.

Let me,

Undo you.

A rush

and then a quiver;

of lips

of thighs

of dormant heartstrings.

And then,

Hush.

Right now

you are beads

of perspiration birthed

from the mounds

of my heaving chest.

Right now

is all I asked for.

"Your eyes. Lives could get lost in those black holes" He said.

"Except yours" she whispered back.

NEW DAY'S EVE

Every frozen moment of you,

I could, tonight, set fire to;

Only to watch you light up my sky-

Fireworks and electric smiles.

Rain down on me, burn my sorrows,

Your love and light on my every tomorrow.

3 a.m.

makes beasts

out of butterflies

and believers

out of the blind.

It rains in song.

The music floods

My rotten cavities;

All vice, gone.

Some evenings choirs

Sing your praise and

Your scent evaporates

From the cracks on my feet.

It rains in song.

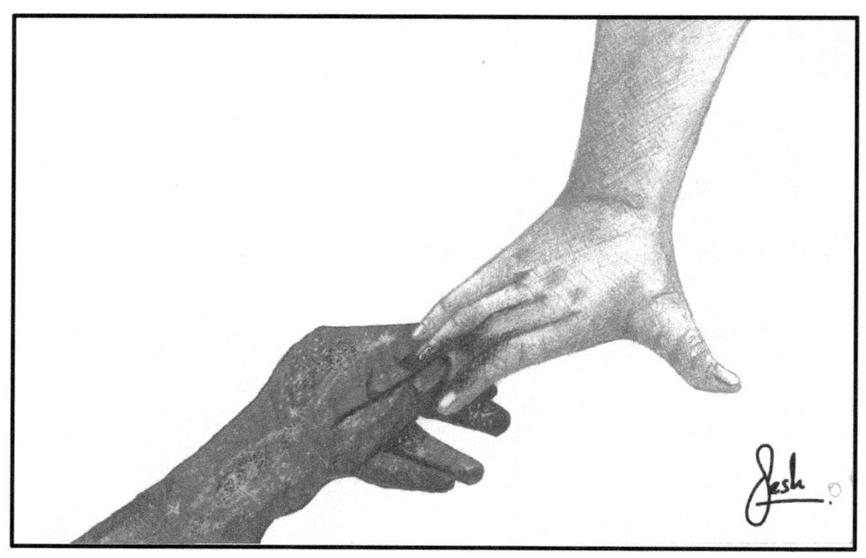

Loss.

The devil. The serpent. The poison apple.

Happiness,

you are such,

unhappiness.

"I don't know what I hate You more for," she said.

"Losing Me, or finding Me."

I gave you passion.

You, left me with poetry.

Only you'd know how to put the pieces back together again:

How everything fits- where the glints and the sharp edges go,

Where the dirt belongs.

Please, be there when I break.

Creator

The deity of his fantasies;

A fire he sparked to life

He knew she'd fade without him

But he cruelly stepped aside.

In case you were looking,

Your hearts still here.

Ever so slightly

Drenched by a tear.

Your scent is tattooed

into my skin.

Now,

I am contaminated,

I am contagious.

I am beautiful.

I can see your music.

It filters in

And dances

In pools;

On my walls, on my bed,

On my mind.,

And it dances too;

On my bed, on my walls

In pools.

But not of music.

Your lips

taste like comfort

and calm seas.

They betray

the pretense

of your face.

You are my comma.

I though, am I only your parentheses.

Everything's been rearranged

Everything's been rearranged

What a storm

What an ocean

What an expanse of spellbinding calm

Not a drop where it used to be

Not a whisper

Not a song.

And so she strung together

Her garland of Unsaids

Swallowed words and choked melodies

That etched years onto her forehead

And everything that they once were

Now lived in a coffin of prose.

We lose what we lose

So that we may become seekers.

That's the thing about storms.

They never come back to check on the destruction

They've left behind.

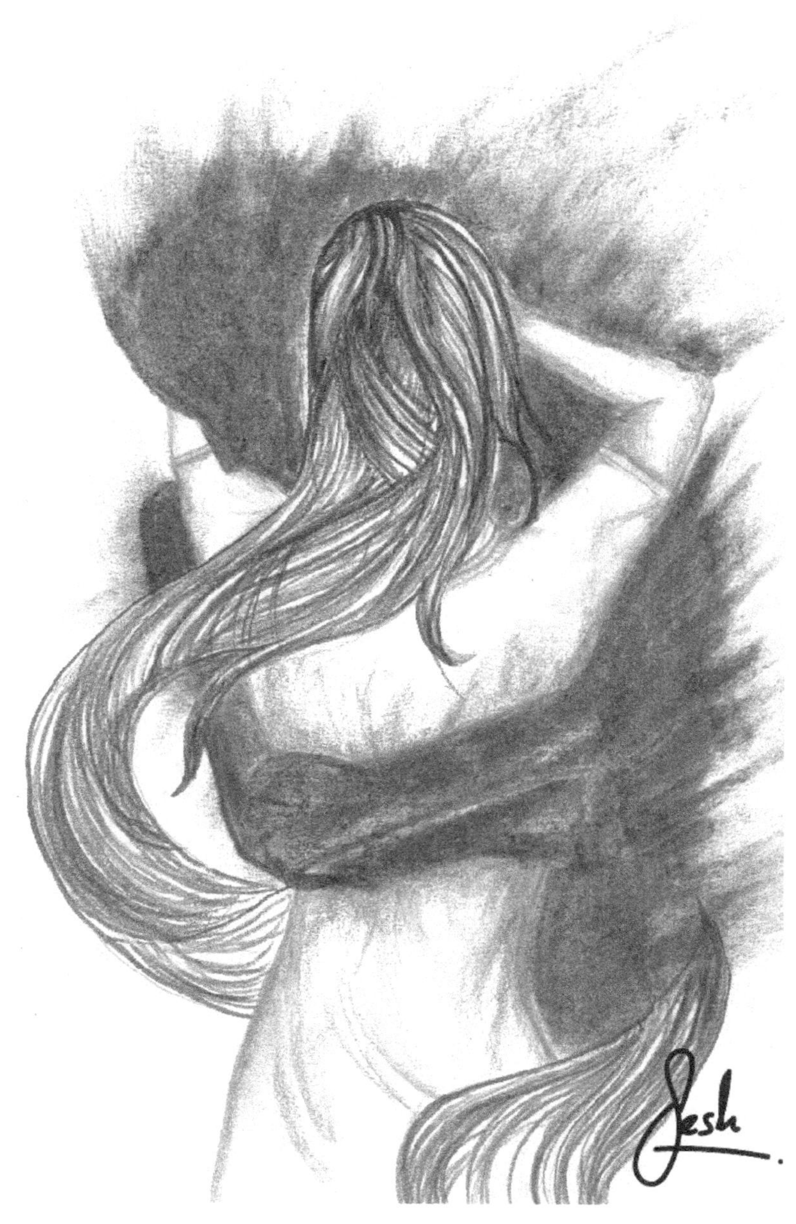

Someday, you will have everything.

Except this.

He preferred to speak now,

to the mask that she wore.

'twas easier to swallow-

her tears were a bore.

As the cautious dawn crept in

and found her in a sorry heap

Every why swirled sadly

in a salty puddle at her feet.

And one night

the pain of living for eternity,

trapped in the tangles of her words

stabbed more than the pain

of living without her.

Today

My wounds scarred

Your thoughts.

Yet,

You tell me

this is not love.

Her smile stayed radiant

with the weight of hope.

But her eyes,

They dimmed a lifetime ago.

Staccato

He left.

In sharp,

painful,

pauses.

Stopping.

Each time

to delight

in a note,

a melody,

a heart beat.

Each time

collecting

a stanza,

an interlude,

a long-drawn hum

of the song,

he shattered.

So that

some day,

he could

compose her

back to life.

In someone else.

Someone.

Else.

Each night she'd weep a lullaby,

Too heavy upon his lids;

He'd wish for wakeful torment

Than her stifling love to keep.

Pillowtalk.

The keeper of all teardrops

Sat fluffy and composed

As the first light seeped in

To disguise what it knows.

Scatter here the ashes of happiness, unlived.

The remnants of promises, unkept.

The knight in shining armour

Saved the damsel in distress

The armour rescued him from her-

No distress. No mess.

The Queen of Hearts

Lay lonely and lost

And laughed

At the joke that was her Name.

We're the stuff that was left behind

When tears forgot to fall.

Someday the tears will know why.

But by then,

There'll be new reasons to cry.

When your nightmares dream,

do they dream

of what

could have been?

Time doesn't heal wounds.

Time creates scab; Layers of hideous tough masks that

pretend to hide the scars and the aching and the red-hot

longing of blood.

Scab is ugly.

It is the static between

Our silences

That narrates

The sorriest of stories

And in time he forgot

where he fit within her arms

so she called him a lesson

to disguise all her scars.

Memories of her were places-

Sprawling vineyards and barren plains

on a shrinking planet

within my veins.

The untouchables song

Name me a name, untamed-

Each letter strung together like

a crown of yet-unnamed thorns.

Name me a name, uncouth-

wails composed of muddy notes like

a serenade to a storm.

Call me a name, anything, whatever

beast your tongue forth brings.

To be a name, to be worth uttering

to you, is everything, understood.

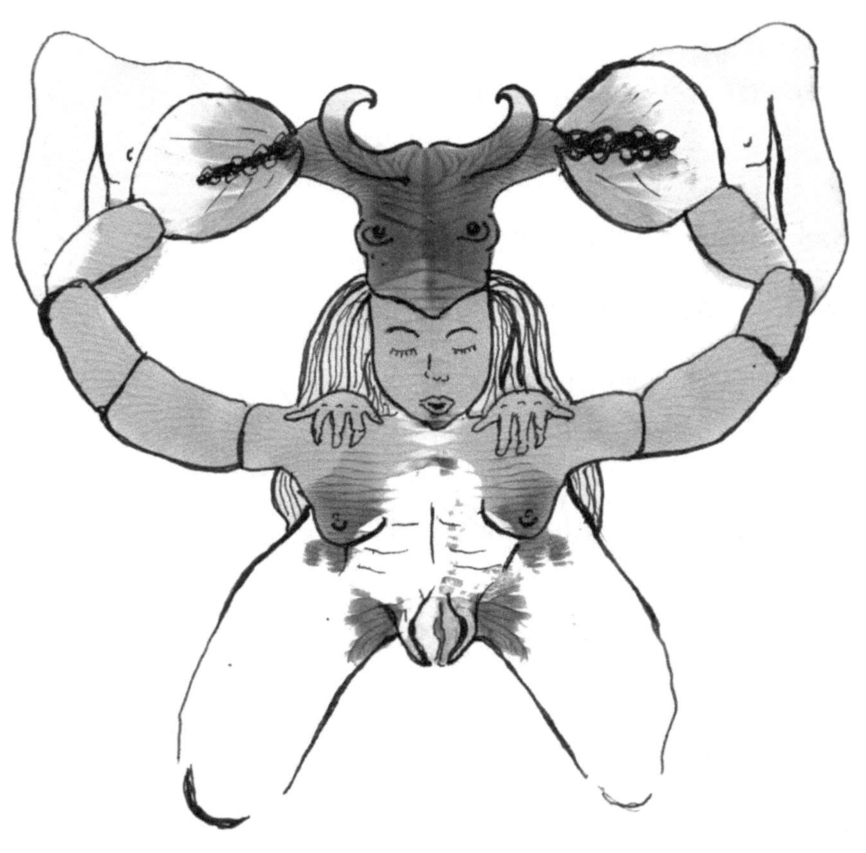

THEY DON'T MATTER BUT THEY DO

I'm the absence of your after-lunch-mint.

The absence of Friday night drinks.

I'm the absence of long to-do lists,

Missed calls and digital-sins.

I'm the absence of life, away from the city,

The absence of stuff sitting pretty.

The absence of things that aren't really things,

The absence that will quietly sting.

Of all the embraces we shared,

The ones that she returned,

Suffocated me the most.

Unwrapped

And this is how you leave me;

Like an exposed secret;

Like the thing you've always wanted,

with its wrapping impatiently undone

and strewn across the floor

on Christmas morning.

Her name-

the lump in my throat,

the knot in my gut,

the incessant howl in the depths where I rot.

Everything & Nothing

You, are a moment

a lifetime,

My soundtrack

to endless nights.

You are ten thousand

excuses

to believe,

to be just right.

But I.

I am but your

Invisible might.

OR

For better OR for worse

In sickness OR in health

To have OR to hold

To Vow OR for now...

Pain on ink,

Charred-soul on paper:

Tears etch songs,

Heartbreaks write fables.

In my dreams You

are different.

Like the pockets of

secrets that hide

within the pleats of

my curtains.

A gust of wind;

The secrets are mine,

and then they are not.

I put the words

in your mouth.

All you did,

was choke on them.

And then you smile-

Enigmatically.

Guiltily.

Sadly.

But I don't.

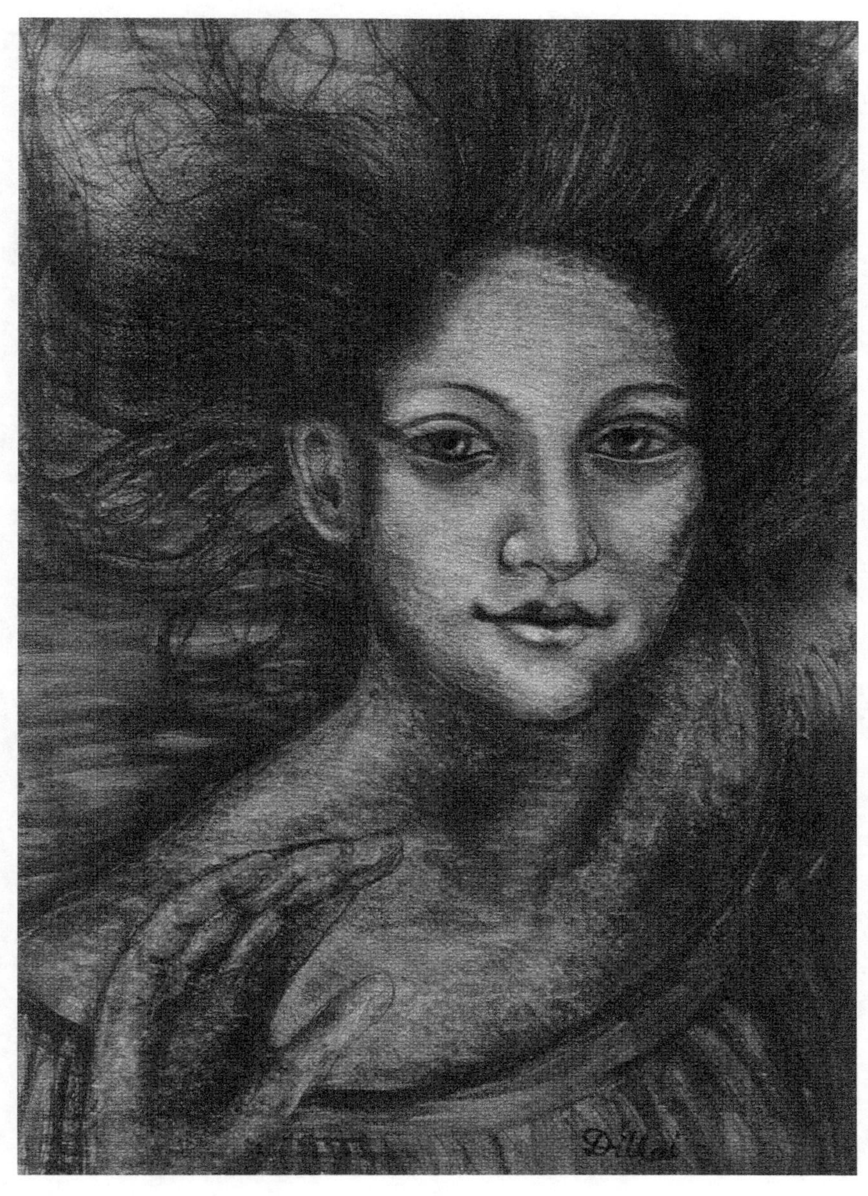

Her Poem.

In her black ink ocean,

time hung still

and sins stood frozen.

Paper shipwrecks

lined her shores,

desire lurking

in their holds.

Mirage

Thoughts of her smelt like coffee and eau de cologne on early

morning sweat.

 Her voice contaminated drive-time static and whispered

lullabies to lonesome pillows.

The expanse of her hips occupied most of my Sunday reading.

She was dust on my windowsill-obstinate about keeping up

reappearances, while I religiously wiped her away.

She'd wipe her ferocious feet on my thick weave of goodbyes

and walk right in. And I'd blink. And she'd smile. And She'd

stay. Away.

TO YOU.

Dear you, untitled,

It's been a long day.

Killed it at work though

Had it my way.

The guys loved my playlist

The tunes were so you.

Maybe, you

had a good one too?

Dear you, untitled,

I'm planning a trip.

Somewhere far away

From the nothing this is.

Not much to miss here

Not much to do.

Maybe you

Should go someplace too.

Dear you, untitled,

It's been a long while.

I watched a wild sunset,

Like a slice of your smile-

I craved your soft fingers

Tracing my brow

Telling me

Maybe, stay awhile more.

Dear you, untitled

The pillows are bare.

The night breeze brings hints

Of the scent of your hair.

My mirage, oasis, magical mare

Forgive me, but

Maybe, untitle me, too.

Here, it is still.

I can hear memories of you

rushing to my pores;

Beads of you escape

through my skin but

I breathe you,

Back in.

Still, I wait here.

Still.

Those tired eyes -

Where are they now?

Charcoal confessionals;

Questioning brows...

Those tired eyes-

They longed for home

They searched in vain

In my hollowed soul

I met them bright-

Those tired eyes.

met them hopeful and hungry,

Fearless and wild.

Where are they now-

Those hungry eyes?

Weary of the hunt

Cautious of the wild.

I failed to see

Deep Into those eyes.

Into the longing

Into the cries.

I thought them crafty

I thought them snide

I thought them lustful,

Her loving eyes.

Do they still seek me-

Those loving eyes?

Do they still weep

For this blind fool's time?

I tired them out,

Those bright black eyes.

I doused the fire

I drowned their nights.

Come back tired eyes

Come back and see

There's a hole in my soul

Where your gaze used to be.

I buried my head in the hollow of her neck; buried my hands,

deeper. The air smelt ugly, the wine was foggy- I was drunk

but I was a believer. I raised my lips and blew in her ear, a

thousand hungry thank yous.' She cradled my head and in a

whistle, said "the lips and the tongues, the pick-me-up's, the

fun, all of it, is free here."

"But the love you're after, you sad old sinner, the love from

here, you pay for."

THE LAST WORD

If I had a conscience, anymore,

It would weep-

For the girl who got lost

for the woman on her knees;

For the blurs and the bruises

That crept up like the night,

For the tears that drenched pillows

Out of sight.

Out of sight.

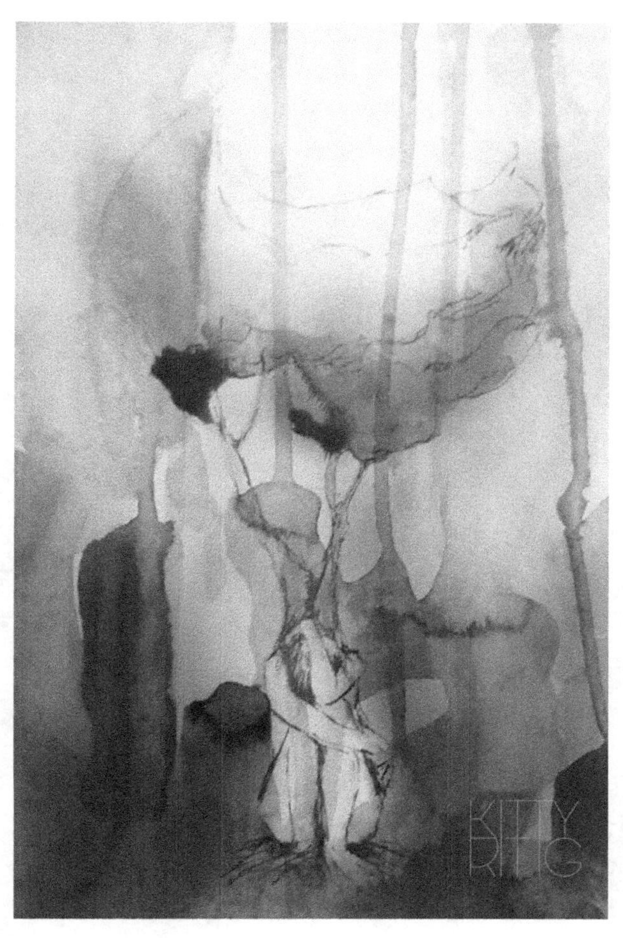

I use your words

to build up walls-

some of them weren't

said at all.

But you

have only let me

undress you.

I am yet

to see you

naked.

Faithful flesh;

Time has left

your scars intact-

In every curve,

In every crack.

Faithful flesh;

I cannot bear

the stench of shame-

Your soul is lost,

Your conscience maimed.

Faithful flesh;

Your swallowed tears

have found their dawn-

I cannot rest.

I cannot rest.

Goddess,

Now made of stone,

As you should have been before.

I can sing your praises now.

Light your lamps,

Shine your throne.

My chisel may have hurt, I know.

But your heart, like mine,

Is now no more.

Goddess,

Now made of stone.

As you should have been before.

You gave me your words,

But never your word.

You wear my love

                              Like a cheap souvenir.

Of all the things

I could not be

I miss being most,

A tear on your cheek.

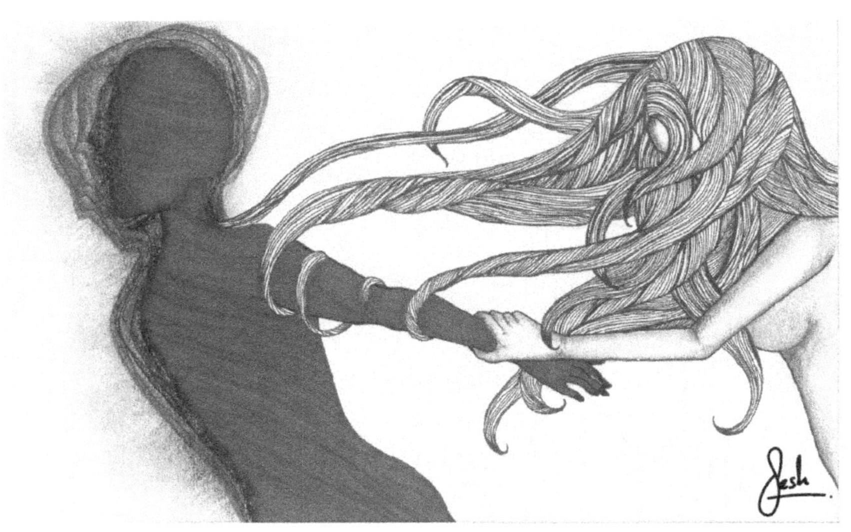

An ode to the words that died.

Swallowed.

Suppressed.

Shy.

THE END.

1.

BAKTHI

('bʌkti/ noun HINDUISM: devotional worship directed to one

supreme deity.)

Stone.Cold.Dream.

Devotions, stream

down my face,

on my knees.

My offerings,

heaped, rotting-

at your feet.

Yet, here I am.

My lamp undying.

And here, I will be.

2.

POOJA

(ˈpuːdʒɑː/ noun HINDUISM/ BUDDHISM :the act of worship.)

Your name:

A sacred thread,

wrapped three times.

A knotted, choking, Prayer.

Chanted,

With reverence, no less

every prescribed hour.

(and sometimes every minute, unprescribed).

3.

DHYAANA

(dɪˈɑːnə/ noun in Hindu and Buddhist practice : profound

meditation)

I could stay here.

Suspended.

Silent.

Forgotten.

Dangling precariously

by a broken memory.

Waiting,

by this sacred fable.

Waiting.

About the Author

Megan Dhakshini is a creative multidisciplinary who has delved into many industries including advertising, creative design, voice acting and singing. Her boutique creative ad shop, The Next Big Think avoids mainstream notions in favor of niche markets. When she isn't caring for her business or her little girl, Megan is writing poetry, perfecting yoga poses or modeling Sarees for a designer friend. POISON APPLE is her debut collection.

INSTAGRAM: @meganpoisonapple

MEDIUM: @megandhakshini

About the Press

UNSOLICITED PRESS is a small publishing house based out of the Pacific Northwest. The team has published more than fifty stunning pieces of poetry, fiction, and creative nonfiction. For more information on the team, visit www.unsolicitedpress.com.